JOY

the mere sense
of living is
JOY
e n o u g h!
emily dickinson

"Set up road signs; put up guideposts.
Take note of the highway, the road that you take"

Jeremiah 31:21

Scrapbooking

Your Spiritual Journey

Inspiring you to tell the stories of God's faithfulness to future generations.

SANDRA L. JOSEPH

"Scrapbooking Your Spiritual Journey"

"Inspiring you to tell the stories of God's faithfulness to future generations"

by Sandra L. Joseph

Published by Reminders Of Faith, Inc

518 Overhead Drive

Moon Township, PA 15108

http://www.remindersoffaith.com

orders@remindersoffaith.com

President: Sandra L. Joseph

Vice President: Kathy Brundage

Art Director: Beth Beiter

Graphic Designer: Dana Thrower

Illustrator: Gina Hurst

Editor: Mary Burke

Scrapbook page layout artists:

Beth Beiter, Corinne French, Chris Pingree, and Marci Whitford

Paper Broker and Advisor: Nancy Guthrie

Photography by Paul Palermo, Palermo Imaging, Warrendale, PA

Sandra's photo by Jill Hart Weaver, Hart Photography, New Brighton, PA

ISBN 0-9748160-0-0

Library of Congress Control Number: 2003099477

Dedication

All the work of this book -- the writing, artwork, and scrapbook pages --

is dedicated to the Lord, giving Him all the honor and glory.

It is not about me, but all about God's faithfulness in my life.

Acknowledgments

Thank you...

- Bill, for being God's gift to me and for living with women all the time. It is fun to be in love with you.

- Alycia, Laryssa and Audrianna for allowing me to pursue what God has called me to do. You are my biggest cheerleaders and the most wonderful daughters ever. I love each one of you very much and am so thankful to be your mother.

- My parents for being wonderful supporters of the dreams that God has given me.

- Kathy Brundage, for being God's answer to my prayer for a detail person, my partner and dear friend.

- Beth Beiter, for being the person God used to teach me about grace, a terrific art director and for always liking me.

- Reminders of Faith investors for heeding the call to believe in what the Lord has called us to do.

LOVE

Song of Solomon 3:4

I have found

the one my heart loves

Love is patient,
love is kind.
It does not envy,
it does not boast,
it is not proud.
It is not rude,
it is not self-seeking,
it is not easily
angered, it keeps no
record of wrongs.
Love does not delight
in evil but rejoices
with the truth.
It always protects,
always trusts,
always hopes,
always perseveres.
Love never fails

I Corinthians 13:4-8

Prayer for our marriage
Jeremiah 32:39

I will give them singleness of heart and action, so that they
will always fear me for their own good and the good of their children
after them. 40 I will make an everlasting covenant
with them: I will never stop doing good to them, and I will
inspire them to fear me, so that they will never turn away
from me. 41 I will rejoice in doing them good and will
assuredly plant them in this land.

Table of Contents

"He has caused His wonders to be remembered."

Psalm 111:4

Forward

I love to scrapbook. It is especially enjoyable with others because it affords the opportunity to share the stories behind each photo. I have shared many photo stories with my good friend, Sandra. I have always appreciated her sincere desire to discover the significance attached to each visual memory. Indeed, our photos are a tangible reminder of what the Lord has done in our lives. Whether times of joy or sorrow, each photo marks a step in our personal journey and reveals the hand of God at work.

Sandra knows of God's hand on her life and has a passion for wanting others to remember the faithfulness of God in their lives as well. So often life overtakes us in the busyness of our schedules that we forget or simply do not take the time to reflect on God's goodness to us, our family, and our friends. As I read this manuscript, how thankful I am for Sandra's vision to lay out an organized plan for incorporating our faith into the memories recorded in our scrapbooks. Plus, seeing this illustrated on actual pages as a creative model to follow is a most helpful resource.

As I have watched Sandra travel the road the Lord has put before her, it has not always been an easy path. It has had detours and roadblocks, but Sandra remains focused on what she knows the Lord is calling her to and as a result has established Reminders of Faith. The magnitude of this endeavor has required her to take her own giant steps of faith and I admire Sandra's willingness to follow God's leading, not certain of where it would ultimately take her. She knows the One she is following and that is good enough for her.

What an inspiring book and valuable resource to encourage and assist each of us in marking our own journey through our scrapbook pages. Thank you, Sandra, for your passion to make this project a reality and for giving us a tool to help us in *Scrapbooking Our Spiritual Journey*.

Carolyn McNicol
Sandra's pastor's wife and friend.

"Future generations will be told about the Lord.
They will proclaim His righteousness to a people
yet unborn – for He has done it."

Psalm 22:30-31

About the Author

My paternal Grandmother scrapbooked her entire life. I remember looking at her scrapbooks every Sunday when we visited her and my Grandpa at their rural farm. When she passed away, each of her children and grandchildren received a scrapbook. These books give each of us a vivid reminder of her life and what was important to her. I too became an avid memory keeper; since my school days, I have created many scrapbooks.

I was introduced to the current scrapbooking trend in 1996 and knew that I had found my life's calling. Since then, God has provided many opportunities for me in the scrapbooking industry. These include a time as National Director of Memories Community, traveling and teaching for 2 years with Memories Expo, serving on various scrapbook advisory boards, and writing and teaching for the scrapbook industry. But always in my heart was God's calling to teach scrapbookers to create reminders of God's faithfulness in their lives. Over and over again, the scriptures tell us to remember what God has done in our lives and to tell others:

"... He commanded our forefathers to teach their children so the next generation would know them, even children yet to be born and they in turn would tell their children. Then they would put their trust in God and not forget His deeds but would keep His commands."

Psalm 78:5-7

This book is the result of many answered prayers and planning by a creative team only the Lord could bring together. The vision may have been placed in my mind first, but is only possible by our Heavenly Father who encourages us to trust Him for everything. I am humbled and honored to be part of what God is doing through Reminders of Faith.

As you will see throughout these pages, I am married to my husband and best friend, Bill. We have 3 wonderful daughters: Alycia, Laryssa and Audrianna. I am involved in my church with MOPS and bible studies. I love to entertain and of course, to scrapbook.

The journey begins...

Journey into Your Spiritual Heritage

Journey into Your Spiritual Heritage

1

Our spiritual journey begins generations before we are born.
Before we take a glimpse of this world or take our first breath,
those who have come before us have set the course for our path.

In order to more fully understand the person you are becoming, it is important to examine the spiritual legacy that has been left by your ancestors. Your heritage makes up who you are; I can see bits and pieces of others as I examine myself. Even if your family does not have a specifically Christian heritage, you can look and see God at work, bringing you to the point you are at now. There is a time that marks the beginning of your journey, but keep in mind that there is still a past that has laid the groundwork for the course your life will take.

"Her children arise
and call her blessed;
her husband also,
and he praises her."

Proverbs 31:28

Bill's Grandparents...
a Heritage from the LORD

Raymond & Alice Joseph

Grandma & Grandpa Joseph reading
to Bill & sister, Mary Alice

Grandma & Grandpa Joseph with Bill & cousins
Phil, Brian, Barb & Brenda 1960

Hopkinton, Iowa
The Joseph Farm

His mercy extends to those who fear him,
from generation to generation. Luke 1:50

Joseph Family Reunion 1996

Before I was born, there was a Godly couple praying for me. Bill grandparents were farmers in Iowa and
they had a deep Christian faith. Before each of their 7 grandchildren were born, they prayed that each
grandchild would follow the call of Christ in their life and that they would marry a Christian so the line of
faith would continue. By the time Bill married me, his Grandmother was gone and his Grandfather was
very old...but I heard the story of how they were praying for Bill's wife since before he was born.

Years later, at a Joseph family reunion, around a camp fire with the cousins, their
spouses and children, Bill's cousin told this story of Grandpa and Grandma Joseph
praying for all of us. He went around the campfire and asked each cousin if
they loved Jesus and then he asked each spouse if they also loved Jesus.
What a testimony to this Godly couple and to their God as each couple responded yes.

He hears the prayer of the righteous. Proverbs 15:29

15

The course for my journey was set years ago by a conservative Christian couple in Hopkinton, Iowa. The moment the coming of their first grandchild was announced, Raymond and Alice Joseph began praying for

I want my children to have a record of Ray and Alice, so they may praise God for working through their prayers. It is important to me that the heritage of our family is passed on. Having a record of the past not only helps

"... You have given me the heritage of those who fear your name."

Psalm 61:5

their grandchildren: that they would grow up to know the Lord, and would marry Christians, continuing the line of faith. My husband, Bill, was the fourth grandchild born, and years later we are able to look at our family -- at seven grandchildren who have all grown up to marry Christians -- and see the rich heritage of prayer and faith left by Ray and Alice. It is powerful for me to think that before I was ever born, a couple in Iowa was praying for me to know the Lord and raise a family that would continue a line of faith started so long ago. In His word the Lord affirms, "He hears the prayer of the righteous." (Proverbs 15:29). The fulfillment of this prayer is a reflection of God's faithfulness to His people.

us to understand ourselves, but also encourages us to pass the baton. When we see the good works of those before us, and the remarkable blessing that has come as a result, we are more likely to carry on the same traditions in our family. We can look at how God has been faithful to our family in the past, and trust that He will continue to be faithful.

My mother is another who laid a great deal of the groundwork for my journey. Barbara Rimer was born during the Depression; she grew up on a farm without luxuries such as jewelry and clothes. As a child, her parents would take her to the feed store to try and get matching cotton feed bags so that her clothes could be made out of a uniform material. Through this time she developed a kind,

Her children arise and call her blessed. Proverbs 31:28

barbara jean manson
1941 Rimersburg PA

barbara jean
w/ baby sandy
1960

My Mother has always been a very soft spoken, elegant woman. I still marvel at how she always has such a regal air about her. She was born during the depression and grew up without many of the finer things of life, but now she is enjoying a beautiful home, pretty jewelry and items she must have dreamed of as a little girl. She always longs to make everything special, especially gifts. Nana always wants to buy something special for each person. I am so thankful for a mother who loved me so much and still treats me in a very loving, gentle way.

gentle spirit, and an enthusi-
asm for making every part of
life special.

My mother now has a
beautiful, regal air about her,
and enjoys jewelry, beautiful
furniture, and other fineries. It
is easy to see how her childhood motivated her to provide
for me a sense of security while
growing up. She taught me a
great deal about making a safe
home for my children and gave
me a pattern of tender, gentle
ways that I strive to emulate.
In the future, when my girls or
their children look at pictures
of my mother, I want them to

To celebrate Mother's Day this year, the girls and I planned a tea party for Nana and Grandma. We sent out invitations, made scones with real whipped cream and cucumber sandwiches. The girls had the most fun going to a bridal store and picking out special dresses to wear at the tea from the ten-dollar rack. Alycia played the piano and Laryssa recited a poem while Audrianna acted the poem out. We then presented their grandmothers with a special teacup to remember our tea party. But I believe that the girls will remember how blessed they are to have grandmothers who share in their lives and from whom they can learn.

know more than what they can see. I want them to know of
her gentleness, her ability to pull the beauty out in others,
and her love for making everything she touches special.

It is not only important to learn about your family's spiritual heritage, but also to honor those who have
provided that heritage for you. In our family, both Bill's
parents and my parents have made a distinct effort to be
together with our family. Through this, my girls have
been allowed to see their family as a complete whole;
even their different sets of grandparents contribute to the

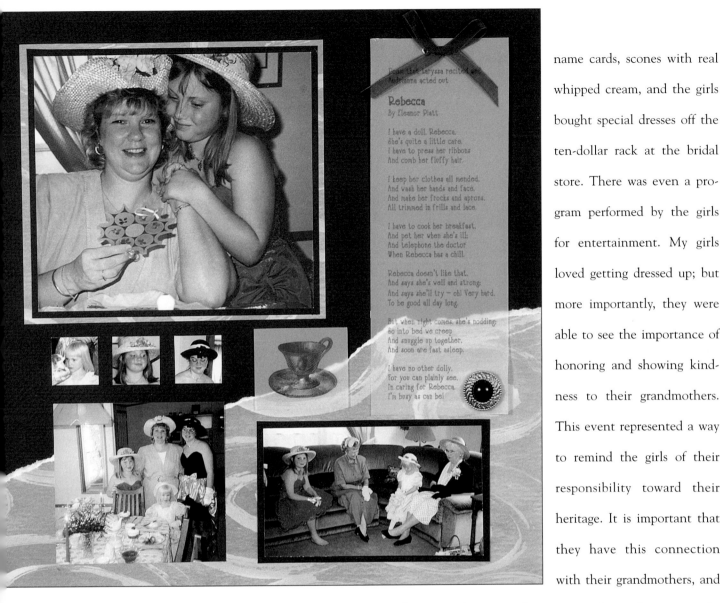

name cards, scones with real whipped cream, and the girls bought special dresses off the ten-dollar rack at the bridal store. There was even a program performed by the girls for entertainment. My girls loved getting dressed up; but more importantly, they were able to see the importance of honoring and showing kindness to their grandmothers. This event represented a way to remind the girls of their responsibility toward their heritage. It is important that they have this connection with their grandmothers, and

sense of unity and security in their lives.

Because of this, we wanted to create an opportunity to honor them in a special way. One Mother's Day, the girls and I made personal invitations, and threw a delightful tea for their grandmothers...and we did it right! We had

that it is documented as a reminder and an example. Scrapbooking your spiritual heritage includes documenting – while you can – those who are the source of that heritage. We need to know the stories of those we love so their story is never lost.

Each of us has a heritage that, with the hand of God, has provided the backdrop for the person we have become. Some may not know of any spiritual history in their family, and some may have a very difficult family background. I think of a woman like Ruth in the Old Testament. She was a Moabite with no spiritual heritage, but the hand of God worked in her life, eventually bringing her into the line of Christ. God does not need a spiritual past to be able to do great things with His people. You don't need a perfect story to be used by God. I don't know what your spiritual heritage is; it may be painful and difficult. When examining your story, I want you to look at the ways God has worked through both the good and bad, both because of and despite your family background.

"Ask the former generation and find out what their fathers learned, for we were born only yesterday, and know nothing and our days on earth are but a shadow. Will they not instruct you and tell you? Will they not bring forth words from their understanding?"

Job 8:8-10

Journeying through God's Plan

Journeying through God's Plan

If we are honest with ourselves, each of us must admit that we have an idea of what our journey should be - how it should play out. Some of the most difficult times in our lives come when we must learn that our actual journey may be radically unlike our plan.

Accepting, growing, and rejoicing in God's plan for our life is sometimes a long, hard process. It is important that we don't skip the hard times when telling our story, for it is often in these times when we most visibly see God's faithfulness. Those who look back on my story need to know that my God pulled me out of anguish and despair. He "heals the brokenhearted and binds up their wounds" (Psalm 147:3); if we trust in Him, He will prove Himself faithful. Documenting the journey through God's plan is telling the entire story. Everyone's path is different, but God works in each of our lives, guiding us faithfully through our journey.

My wedding was an accumulation of great expectations, love, excitement and intense feelings. My expectations...there is not a princess in a fairy-tale whose anticipations could match mine. I knew that marriage would satisfy my wants and longings built up over a lifetime. It would be perfect. I was so eager to begin a family with Bill; in my mind, it was as if the journey was finally beginning. While dating, Bill and I were a model Christian couple, and I need to know what He started with. I want them to be able to see my mindset, my hopes and my thoughts as they look at these pages.

Soon after our wedding, I had to make some huge adjustments to my picture of what my life, my journey, would be. It was already time for a bump in the road that I thought would be so smooth. After our weeklong honeymoon, we returned home and opened our gifts at my parents' house. My

"'For I know the plans I have for you,' declares the Lord, 'plans to prosper you and not to harm you, plans to give you hope and a future.'"
Jeremiah 29:11

thought that since we had done it right, we deserved to have an ideal life together. Our wedding pictures represent that outlook to me.

It is important that when my girls look at those photographs in fifty years, they see more than my outdated wedding dress and hairstyles of the past. I want to document all the feelings and expectations that went into that day. If others are to see how God has worked in my life, they mother commented that I was remarkably thin; it turns out I had dropped 14 pounds in one week. We went to our new apartment, but on Sunday I was feeling desperately tired and ill. We went to the hospital. At first I was afraid that doctors and nurses would be angry at me for wasting their time. I was tired and thirsty; I didn't see how this required a trip to the emergency room. Soon we had become the hospital's Celebrity Couple: the bridegroom and his bride who had an

Promise

This is the day I have waited and dreamed of all my life. I remember playing wedding dress up as a little girl, always desiring to be the bride. As I grew up I not only wanted to just the bride, I wanted to be loved by the man the Lord had chosen for me. Of course, everything was to be just perfect but God had different plans — our outdoor wedding had to become an indoor wedding due to rain, our cake toppled and the instead of driving away in a cute sports car, we left in a station wagon Bill had bought so "we could haul things". But I decided not to let any of those things take away from my happiness and excitement. Our pastor told me that he thought I was a glowing beautiful bride and that is truly how I felt — happy, excited, love, and great expectations. I imagined that once the wedding ceremony was over that we would then live "Happily Every After", little did I know that day what would happen in a few days to shake my dreams.

. . . I found the one my heart loves
Song of Solomon 3:4

Heirs together of the grace of life.
1 Peter 3:7

I will rejoice greatly
in the Lord
My Soul will exalt
in my God
For He has
clothed me with
garments
of Salvation
He has
wrapped me
with a robe of
righteousness
As a bridgeroom
decks himself
with a garland
And a bride
adorns herself
with her jewels

Isaiah 61:10

William & Sandra

September 5, 1981

I, Bill, take you Sandy as my lawful wedded wife,
to be joined together by God as one flesh, and I
do promise and covenant before God and these
witnesses, to forsake all others, cleave to and
abide with only you as long as we both shall live.

I will provide and care for you, honor and cherish
you, seek to love you as Christ loved the church
and gave Himself for it, be the head of our home
even as Christ is the head of the church, and
prayerfully guide our lives as joint heirs of the
grace of eternal life.

I, Sandy, take you Bill as my lawful wedded
husband, to be joined together by God as one
flesh and I do promise and covenant before God
and these witnesses, to forsake all others, cleave
to and abide with only you as long as we both
shall live.

I will love you, honor you faithfully with respect,
meet your needs to the best of ability. Because
of God's love dwelling in me, I will obey you with
submisssion as the church obeys Christ, and
prayerfully follow you as joint heirs of the grace
of eternal life.

800+ blood sugar count (a normal count being 80-100) and signs of insulin-dependent diabetes.

A week earlier, we had vowed to each other, "in sickness and in health." Those vows were quickly put into a whole new perspective. The dream came crashing down around me, and I spent eight days in the hospital dealing with loneliness, frustration, and anger toward God. This was a time when I had to learn the meaning of God's sovereignty — beyond the clichés. I could not understand why God would do this to Bill and me. We had done everything right. This was a difficult time in my journey, and I want those who come after me to understand that I struggled. It was more

Documenting your spiritual journey means recording your low points as well as your high points. My plan for my life had been taken away and I couldn't understand why; however, by showing this time in my life to future generations, I am showing God's faithfulness and ability to pull me out of the very hardest of times.

Fast forward our lives through many years of difficulty and disappointment and you come to a photograph of Bill and me. We received a coupon in the mail for a free family portrait. After the family pictures were taken, the photographer asked whether Bill and I wanted to take a portrait. It brings back a bittersweet memory. This was a

"Yet I am always with you; you hold me
by my right hand. You guide me with your
counsel and afterward you will take me into glory."
Psalm 73:23

than the challenge of accepting a disease such as diabetes, even more than accepting a marriage that may not live up to my expectations. I had to accept a God who would take my dreams away from me after I had done everything right.

time of intense pain and suffering in our marriage; however, we took the picture as a symbol of our commitment to our family, despite our troubles. We believed that God would be faithful and restore our relationship and our

LORD?

Lord,

Today, five weeks after our wedding, we took the wilted flowers off the trellis that Bill built for us to stand under during our wedding ceremony.

After everything that has happened, I feel like one of these ugly wilted flowers. It isn't supposed to be like this ... I was expecting to be a happy, carefree, in-love newlywed, but now I am dealing with insulin shots, stupid diets, doctors and not feeling good.

I thought You would bless us because we tried so hard to do what You wanted and commanded us to do. It really seems unfair, especially as I watch our other friends get married and not have to struggle with these kinds of things. No one really understands how I feel, not even Bill.

I remember my Dad's tears at my bedside in Intensive Care, wishing it could have been him instead of me. In all honesty, I wish it could have been anyone but me! I expected "Happily Ever After," not this.

But I am thankful, Lord, that I can come to You with my honest feelings. I do appreciate the support that we have from our families. My parents have helped, but without intruding wanting us to be established as a married couple. And I know that Bill's parents, even though they live far away, have been praying for us.

Please help me to deal with all of this and to not give up.

family. We were committed to the path the Lord had for us, whether or not it was what we had expected. It would be easy to look at this picture and see a happy couple; but looking back now, it means so much more. When someone looks at this scrapbook page, I want him or her to see more than another couple. This picture represents the pain and agony of that time, but also symbolizes our commitment to the future. It reminds me that God faithfully brought us through those painful circumstances and rebuilt our relationship, reestablishing great love, excitement and joy.

"A righteous man may have many troubles,
but the Lord delivers him from them all."
Psalm 34:19

Journey into God's Calling

Journey into God's Calling

Picture a warm summer night. You are a child playing outside in the neighborhood when you hear a voice calling you home. This image brings a sense of warmth and comfort to me - a sense of security in knowing I belong somewhere. This is how I see God's calling.

So often, like a child called home from playing outside, we fight against God's calling. So many of us think that we know better, and if only we could do it our way, we would find real happiness. When we finally give in and respond to His calling, there is so much comfort in knowing and accepting our true place of belonging. A large part of your journey through God's plan includes the process of discerning God's calling for you. This is an important part of the spiritual journey; it needs to be documented so that the future generations can see how God used you in His plan. Each of us has special gifts and talents that God can use specifically to His glory; it is only when we match our gifts to God's purpose that we can enjoy true satisfaction in our work. Let those who look back on your scrapbooks see more than your activity or job; make sure they understand that God's faithfulness is evident in your ability to discern His calling in your life.

May the favor of the Lord our God rest upon us. Establish the

work of our hands for us - yes, establish the work of our hands.

Bill has always been one of the most gifted men I know he can do anything... rebuild an engine, program a computer, be a great Dad to girls, and love a high maintenance wife. Yet, for such a long time he experienced such frustration in his work. I have never seen him happier than when he was building our house. After that, he started his own business, Wm Joseph Contracting. This undertaking allows Bill to use his aptitude for working with his hands, for leading others who work with him as well as feeling the satisfaction from doing what God created him to do.

PSALM 127:1

UNLESS THE LORD BUILDS THE HOUSE, THE BUILDERS LABOR IN VAIN.

Bill the Builder

"We have different gifts according to the grace given to us."
Romans 12:6

During vacation, when we go to the beach, my husband, Bill, delights in building the largest, most intricate sandcastle that can be built in a day. As I look back on these pictures now, they remind me of so much more than our trips to the beach. They remind me of a process that took place in our lives years later.

My husband is one of the most talented men I have ever known. He can figure out how to do anything. However, because of his many talents it was hard for him to focus on his greatest gift - his calling. In his attempts to find success, he tried many things that were not his calling. A part of our struggle for many years came from this struggle in Bill's life. In the midst of a truly broken time, he started working with remodeling homes and kitchen installations. He discovered not only an aptitude for working with his hands, and a tal-

Sandcastles

2002 North Carolina

1799 ocean city NJ

Sandcastles of FUN!
Once again, Daddy could not be content to sit on the beach and read, he has to be doing something with his hands. He sees his job at the beach to build the biggest sandcastle that can be possibly built from the girls' simple sand toys. A sandcastle that will be much admired by people who stroll by and then will be washed away by the tide in the evening. Bill is so good at creating with his hands; he can design and build a house even out of sand.

ent for leading others who worked with him, but also a satisfaction in his job.

In Psalm 90:17, the writer pleads for the Lord to "establish the work of our hands for us." This verse reminds me of Bill, because when you are doing what God has called

1989 ocean city NJ

now, I see that as a reflection of God's calling in his life many years ago, before we had even discerned what it would be. It is so important to me that when others look at these scrapbook pages of Bill, that they understand that they are a reflection of this struggle and triumph in his life. They exhibit God's faithfulness in beginning to show Bill his calling years ago. Throughout our lives, God is faithful to call us — to lead us on our journey. Document for the future generations your story of how God has called you, and the process you under-

you to do, you will find fulfillment and inner success, but as long as you struggle against His plan you will struggle to find contentment in your work.

Throughout those years, Bill found such pleasure working with his hands to build sandcastles. Looking back

went to discern and accept that calling.

One thing special about women is that our lives are often divided into stages; in each stage there may be a different calling for your life. While my girls were young, my calling was to be a full-time, stay-at-home mother to them.

However, once they had grown and gone to school, it was time for me to listen and see if God had another calling for this new stage in my life. Often, the acceptance of God's calling requires a huge leap of faith on our part.

"Unless the Lord builds the house, its builders labor in vain."

Psalm 127:1a

I have always been meticulous about keeping my photographs. Little did I know where that would eventually lead me! During the hard financial times in our past, I was told that I should just take any job I could find; I even applied for a receptionist position. I wasn't hired...God had bigger plans. The Lord gave me the idea to start a scrapbooking association. This was before people had even heard of scrapbooking, and when I went to the small business co-op, they looked at me like I was crazy. However, the Lord provided. Because of my diabetes, and the fact that I am a rare case of a patient who is actually allergic to insulin, I qualified for a $10,000 grant. Even though Bill and I were deeply in debt, I took that grant money and rented the Pittsburgh Expo-Mart, for $16,000. Everyone thought I was crazy, and I had no idea how I would do it,

but I knew this was God's plan. I took a step of faith, and I was scared, but God provided. In April of 2000 we had a scrapbooking convention with 1700 women from 13 different states. One thing led to another; I started doing other shows, and I received the opportunity to become the National Director for Memories Community. I now teach, write, and interact with those in the scrapbooking industry. God continues to work and has been faithful even in the times that I doubted him.

My calling is more than scrapbooking, but to tell God's people that they need to leave records of His faithfulness. Documenting my story is more than telling my grandchildren that I worked in this industry; they need to see the amazing ways in which God provided. The verse I have now claimed as I continue in my work is Habakkuk 1:5b, "For I am going to do something in your days that you would not believe, even if you were told."

Our daughter, Laryssa is incredibly gifted with children. She has a heart that draws children to her, and she is often in demand for baby-sitting, teaching Sunday school, and teaching Vacation Bible school. She spent one summer teaching for Child Evangelism Fellowship. What joy it gave her to be able to use her gifts. Her future children need to see how God was faithful to reveal her ability to work with

Scrapbooking, My Career

For I know the plans I have for you," declares the Lord, "plans to prosper you and not to harm you, plans to give you hope and a future.

Jeremiah 29:11

Heart's Treasures: 1998-1999
Hosted a small local scrap-booking group in a coffee house, then in my home. Sold scrapbook supplies out of our dining room.

Tri-State Scrapbooking
1999-2001, Owner
Produced Pittsburgh Scrapbook Convention. 1700 attendance from 13 different states. Also, hosted the Caribbean Scrapbook Cruise.

Memories Community
2001-2003, National Director
Traveled to 14 Memories Expos throughout the United States promoting Memories Community, hosting crops, teaching retail trainings, and networking within the scrapbook industry.

Joel 1:3
Tell it to your children, and let your children tell it to their children, and their children to the next generation.

Psalm 22:30-31
...future generations will be told about the Lord. They will proclaim His righteousness to a people yet unborn - for He has done it.

Reminders of Faith, Inc.
2003, President
I am just walking through the doors the Lord is opening for us by writing, talking, networking, marketing, and always thinking of the next step.

"Whether you turn to the right or to the left, your ears will hear a voice behind you, saying, 'This is the way; walk in it.'"

Isaiah 30:21

children, and provide this opportunity for her to use her gift. It was such a blessing for us to see her ministering to young children throughout our county, telling Bible stories and developing relationships. Also, I must add that she made a scrapbook of her entire CEF experience! We have studied Laryssa so that we can help guide her into her calling; it will be exciting to watch her continue to use those talents throughout her life. Years from now it will be such a blessing to look back on these pages and reflect on how God was faithful in providing her with gifts and occasions to use them. What a blessing that we, as parents, have the privilege to help begin our children on their spiritual journey!

"I have no greater joy than to hear that my children are walking in the truth."

3 John 4

Journeying with Your Family

Journeying with 4 Your Family

God blesses us by providing other people to travel with us
on our spiritual journey. For many of us, our family travels
the road with us at the high points and low points of our life.

It is essential that we document different aspects of our familial relationships so that future generations can see the special qualities of each. As our journey continues, we find more people with whom we travel. Our children are a special reflection to Bill and me of our relationship and our love for each other. The combination of the two of us has allowed for the creation of each of these girls. I can not imagine my journey without my family, and I thank God for his faithfulness in providing such wonderful relationships to help me along my journey.

Alycia Jean

Alycia – Truthful
Jean – God is Gracious
Age: 2, November 1986

You are special because you made me a mother. Everything was a first with you. I will never forget how
strongly I loved you even before you were born and how I still am amazed at the love I have for you.
We had this photo taken as a surprise for your Daddy for Christmas but it turned out so good that the photographer
put it up outside his shop in the mall. Others saw it and told your Dad, so it was not a surprise.
I love this picture of you and me because it portrays all the rich feelings I feel about being a Mother.

A mother's relationship with her daughter is a very unique and special one. I have known many kinds of love, but the most intense love I have ever felt came through the

young". Not only did I finally glimpse the nature of God's love, but also I was given a new understanding and assurance of the Lord's relationship with a parent. His faithful-

"The promise is for you and your children and for all who are far off - for all whom the Lord our God will call"
Acts 2:39

birth of our three daughters, Alycia, Laryssa, and Audrianna. This love surprised me by how quickly and deeply it settled into my heart. I learned to love our daughters in an unselfish, giving way, knowing that I would do anything necessary for these girls. One of the many great things about this relationship is that it gave me a new understanding of God's love for us. Until I had children, even though I had a husband, my focus was often on myself. It was easy for me to be self-involved. Once I had children, I began to mature in a new way, becoming able to take the focus off myself and become more who God was calling me to be. It wasn't until I reached this point that I could understand in even the tiniest fraction the nature of God's unconditional love. Isaiah 40:11 speaks of how the Lord is a Shepherd who "gently leads those that have

ness continues in His love, and His kindness in giving me new understandings of that love. These photos are so much more than beautiful, professionally taken pictures. To me, they represent a new understanding and fullness of love.

There is a special relationship not only between a mother and her daughters, but also between a father and his daughters. I believe that it takes a very special man to be able to be a good father - a daddy - to girls. A girl needs a father who will make her feel special, twirl her around in her dress-up dresses, teach her to play basketball, and let her snuggle up to him. A good father has to be many things at all times. Bill has been able to do all this without ever feeling like he was missing out because he doesn't have a son. As I look at pictures of Bill with the girls, I remember times when he happily played Prince Charming for

Laryssa Lynn

How I wanted another daughter ... I was so happy when in the delivery room I heard it was another little girl. From the moment you came into my life, my love for you has always been very deep as well as sweet. I gave you my middle name so you would know how special you are to me. It has been a joy watching many of my character traits in you and yet I cringe when I see my faults show through. You are the perfect middle daughter, valuing the fact that you are the only one with an older and younger sister. Daddy wanted us to get this photo taken and you were a natural model. Your bright smile in this photo matches the meaning of your name and reminds me of how often you make me laugh.

Laryssa – Cheerful,   Lynn – Pretty one
Age: 3, Photo taken Spring 1990

Audrianna Elizabeth

What a **special gift** you have been to me as my youngest daughter. I have so enjoyed having you as the younger one especially as the girls got older. It has been so dear to still have a **little girl** in our home. Throughout your baby and preschool days, you and I were **buddies**; we had so much fun together (and we still do).
I was so glad when God gave a third daughter. I thought that 3 sisters would be so much fun, and it has been such a **blessing**.
We got this photo taken for Daddy. He gave me the ring you see on my pinky for our 10th anniversary while I was pregnant with you.

Age 4, Fall 1996

Audrianna - Noble Strength
Elizabeth - Consecrated to God

MY DAD

MY DAD

Love, Audrianna Joseph on Father's Day, June 2003

If you know someone who's awfully tall,
Who's always bonking his head on walls.

Who likes to fix things big and small
Who peoples kitchens does install.

Who can often be a goof-ball,
Who in the shower stalls

If you know someone who's jokes are bad,
Then you probably know my nice Dad!

My Dad is cool,

Mean he is not,

So see, I love my Dad a lot!

"He will turn the hearts of the fathers to their children and the hearts of the children to their fathers."

Malachi 4:6

that should be documented. He is a gentle, loving father who is able to enjoy each daughter for the gifts and abilities that she has. God has been faithful in giving the girls such a wonderful father, and in giving him patience, tenderness and an unending supply of love while living outnumbered in a household of women!

Some relationships are just special; as

Beaver County Christian School
Christmas Dance
December 2001

Special Date with Daddy...

Daddy escorted Alycia and Laryssa to the Christmas dance this year. He took them out to dinner at The Grand Valley Inn and then took them to the dance. He went in for photos and then promptly left as the girls were having fun with their friends.
He felt very proud of his daughters and the fact that they were willing to be escorted by their Dad.
He even wore his boutonniere to church the next day knowing that people would ask why he had it.
He was so proud to tell others of his special date with his daughters.

Audrianna when she wanted to be Cinderella. One year, he got dressed up and took the girls' out to dinner as their date to the school Christmas dance, and then dropped them off at the school to enjoy their evening. As others look back at these pictures, I want them to know the scope of Bill's relationship with his girls. These are not just any father-daughter relationships, but each has special nature

you look at certain people, you know that the Lord created your relationship to fit perfectly. That is the way I feel about my relationship with my Dad. Our earthly Fathers are our first glimpse of how we will relate with our Heavenly Father. My earthly Father has always been strong yet gentle with solid ideas of right and wrong. He is always humming or singing whatever song is in his mind that day.

I get my love of reading and buying books from him. Most of all, he has always been someone I could go to whenever I needed someone to listen to me, pray for me, and give me advice. This helped me learn over the years that I could go to my heavenly Father in the same way; he would be there to listen to me and to provide advice through His word, the Bible. It is hard to imagine what my life will be like when my father goes to heaven and I am left without this valuable relationship in my life. Yet, I know that I have my relationship with my heavenly father to fulfill this need until I can join my Dad in heaven. I will also have my scrapbooks — reminding me of so many dear memories — to help carry me through until I join him.

I know of the possible struggles with the oldest child when a younger sibling joins the family. When I brought our second daughter, Laryssa, home from the hospital, it was such a joy to see that her two and a half year old sister, Alycia, acted with kindness toward her. Laryssa was often ill, and cried frequently. One time I couldn't get to her right away; when I entered the room I saw that

always daddy's girl

Wedding Day September 5th 1981

Dad & Sandy 1962

Gardening together in Clarion, PA

- Gentle
- Reader
- Strong
- Prayerful
- Smart
- History Lover
- Always singing, humming or whistling

My Dad has always been someone very special to me. He could do amazing things when I was little, like lift me off the ground when I was hanging onto his arms. He had big strong fingers (which he always told me came from milking cows) but an even bigger soft spot in his heart towards me. When I was 4 or 5, I crawled up into his lap and he helped me ask Jesus into my heart. I remember traveling with him on summer days, going out to Kentucky Fried Chicken together. I still recall him getting locked out of the house while waiting for me to return from a walk with a boy. I am told that I get my stubbornness and many other characteristics from him.

When I was diagnosed with diabetes only days after my wedding, I remember his words spoken with tears, of how he wished it were him instead of his daughter. He has always been one of my favorite people to talk to, and through out my years I have relied on his support. I love the fact that when our conversation is done or he doesn't know what else to say, he just breaks into prayer.

I am so thankful for my Dad. It means so much to me to know that I will always be His girl.

DADDY'S GIRLS

Anyone can be a father, but it takes
someone special to be a **Daddy**.

He will turn the **hearts** of the father to their children
and the **hearts** of the children to their fathers.

Malachi 4:6

Alycia had brought out all her stuffed animals and laid them around Laryssa trying to make her happy. She even held out her most precious friend - a stuffed bunny affectionately called "Bubba" - to her screaming sister in an attempt to help. As a mother, my desire is to facilitate that sort of kindness toward each other in our home.

I have been a real stickler about making our home a safe place, both emotionally and relationally. If the girls get beat up by the world, or don't feel like they quite fit in, I want them to know that they can come home to a place of kindness and love. Through the years, it's been fun watching their little acts of kindness to each other. Sisters are a special variety of friend. They will continue on their journey together throughout their lives, and they know the same little quirks and characteristics of our family. I want to document these kindnesses, because they reflect the depth of security the girls have been able to find in their relationships with each other. Also, how they

Family

Love

When I was pregnant with Audrianna, everyone kept assuming that I must want a little boy since we already had 2 girls. But my heart's desire was to have another girl. I thought 3 sisters would be so much fun. Never having a sister, I always though that the relationship between sisters was something special. Alycia and Laryssa both wanted another girl as well. The day I delivered Audrianna, Alycia had talked herself into believing it was a boy so she wouldn't be disappointed, but when we called them with the news she cried with tears of joy. Laryssa had told us all along that the baby was a girl because she supposedly saw a bow in the baby's hair in a sonogram picture. From the moment Alycia and Laryssa saw Audrianna there began a special bond that sometimes makes me jealous. I am so glad that you will always have each other to share your joys and tears. God gave you to each other and I pray that your bond as sisters will always be close.

Love one another. As I have loved you so you must love one another.
John 13:34

How do people make it through life without a sister?
~ Sara Corpening

"Be kind and compassionate to one another, forgiving each other, just as in Christ God forgave you."

Ephesians 4:32

Sister's Love

Memories of childhood may someday fade
But never the special games we played
Though our tea party days have come to an end
You're always my sister, always my friend.
(Taken from a picture hanging on my wall of 3 little girls having a tea party, a gift from Bill.)

relate to each other reflects how they interact with the world. I have had people tell me how kind my girls are, and in my mind I can trace this back to their ability to be kind to each other. God has blessed our family with the gifts of love and kindness. That is something to be celebrated and documented so that one day Alycia, Laryssa, and Audriana's children can look back on their mother's relationships as a model for their own.

"He tends his flock like a shepherd; He gathers the lambs in his arms and carries them close to His heart; He gently leads those that have young."

Isaiah 40:11

The Everyday Journey

The Everyday Journey

God is faithful not only in the big decisions, plans, and occasions. He also guides us through the everyday journey in a way that we never realize.

We are taken back by anything that goes wrong. Imagine if we woke up one morning and the sun never came up; the earth simply stopped moving. We trust God for everyday things and live without realizing the showers of blessings we receive daily. Documenting our spiritual journey includes recognizing God for these things: the work of our hands, the world around us, and the things we do daily without ever thinking.

Sleep

It gives me great peace to see my family sleeping. These pictures make me feel comforted for I know that my family felt secure and safe to fall soundly asleep.

I will lie down and sleep in peace, for you alone, O Lord , make me dwell in safety. Psalm 4:8

He grants sleep to those he loves.Psalm 127:2

"Therefore my heart is glad and my tongue rejoices;
my body also will rest secure."

Psalm 16:9

Every journey requires a time of rest. Sleep is an amazing gift, a break from the trials and excitements of daily living. I have found that I can only sleep well if I am at peace; I don't rest well when something is bothering me

There are times, spiritually, when I think God forces us to rest. He knows our limits better than we do. It is a blessing to have a God that both knows and cares about something that seems so small. Documenting our spiritual journey

"He has shown kindness by giving you rain from heaven and crops in their seasons; He provides you with plenty of food and fills your hearts with joy."

Acts 14:17b

or hurting me. You only sleep well when you feel secure. A part of God's faithfulness to us is in providing that security and ability to sleep. Psalm 127:2 tells us, "He grants sleep to those he loves." The writer of Psalm 4:8 confidently says, "I will lie down and sleep in peace, for you alone, O Lord, make me dwell in safety." Looking at these pictures adds to my sense of peace, for I know that my family felt secure enough to fall soundly asleep. It breaks my heart to think of all those in the world who sleep in fear. I know I have been blessed because my family and I can sleep in peace.

We don't always want to sleep. I think of a young child kicking and screaming all the way to the bedroom.

includes the things that happen every day. Think about your life and be reminded of the simple ways that God provides for and blesses you a thousand times every day. Too often we never consider these things.

Everyday blessings include life's little joyous surprises that we quickly forget about as we move on. My daughter, Audrianna, is in middle school, a time between the worlds of girlhood and womanhood. Not long ago, I received a postcard from the new Hallmark store in our area to enter a drawing for free American Girl™ dolls. I found out she had won, and decided to make something special of it. I called her at school and got her out of class to tell her.

Psalm 145:9
The Lord is
Good to all;

He has
compassion
on all He
has made.

Audrianna's
American Girl Dolls

Win all seven
American Girl Mini Dolls and
a Keep-in-Touch Kit!

In the mail, I received a postcard from the new Hallmark store to enter a drawing for free American Girl™ dolls. I saved the postcard for a month, and actually remembered to take it to the store on the Saturday that we could enter. I was surprised when on Monday I got a phone call telling me that Audrianna had won. I called her at school and got her out of class to tell her that she won. After she got home from school we went and picked up the dolls. As we got in the car to leave, we prayed thanking God for remembering Audrianna in such a special way. God knew that at this time in her life as a fifth grader, she needed something to make her feel special.

PUMPKINS

As long as the earth endures, seedtime and **harvest**, cold and heat, summer and winter, day and night will never cease.
Genesis 8:22

Every fall, we enjoy picking, cleaning (well, maybe not the cleaning part) and carving our pumpkins. Daddy always has to help finish cleaning out the final seeds. Our pumpkins seem to come alive after we give them eyes, noses and mouths, sometimes Daddy even helps us give them special personalities like Bert and Ernie.

Bert and Ernie.

> "The Lord is compassionate and gracious,
> slow to anger, abounding in love."
> Psalm 103:8

After she got home we went and picked up the dolls. As we got in the car to leave we prayed together. I wanted to thank God for providing this seemingly small blessing to make her feel special for a day. It was what she needed at that point in her life. In the scriptures we often read that the Lord looked down and had compassion on His people. He had compassion on the Israelites. Jesus had compassion and fed the 5,000. Psalm 103:13 says that, "As a father has compassion on his children, so the Lord has compassion on those who fear him." God has just as much compassion on an 11-year-old girl who may be struggling through a difficult time in life as he did for the Isrealites. Document these small events so you can look back at them as blessings, and remember them for what they are: reminders of God's faithfulness.

Christmas COOKIES

CHRISTMAS COOKIE TRADITION

Each year we enjoy baking our favorite Christmas Cookies. Some years, we do all the baking in one day ...what a mess the kitchen becomes. We always enjoy when Papa and Nana come to help. Each of us have our favorites...

- *Chocolate Kiss Cookies*
- *Peanut Butter Balls*
- *Pretzels with Chocolate Kisses*
- *Seven layer Cookies*
- *Nana's Fudge*
- *Decorated Sugar Cookies*

The Sugar cookies were always the favorite when the girls were little because they loved to decorate them. Now, they insist that they don't want to do sugar cookies because they know there will be a huge mess to clean up afterwards.

nana + pa pa

yummy!

sugar cookie fun!

'99 12 22

Christmas 1999

The **greatest gift** of this Christmas was God's faithfulness to us in the midst of our broken lives. Through a series of events, Bill & I had been through very rough times financially, as well as in our relationship. But when Christmas came, it reminded us of God's promise to redeem our situation for His glory. God blessed us with His peace & the knowledge we were doing His will.

The Lord is close to the brokenhearted and saves those who are crushed in spirit. Psalm 34:18

Dear Mommy & Daddy,

Thank you for everything you do for me! I know that somedays I don't appreciate it but I really do! I know we have had a hard year but God isn't through yet! Don't give up! I am glad you are my parents, I wouldn't want anyone else!

I love you!

Merry Christmas!!

Your Daughter,

Alycia Jean

One year I made a scrapbook of every event of the year and I noticed that every year is very much like the prior ones. Sometimes our lives may seem routine, but this must help our sense of security. We count on the seasons turning, the calendar moving on. Our year is full of events from holidays and birthdays to the yearly school jog-o-thon. Traditions, no matter how small, are worth celebrating. I think of how we always have ham for Easter and turkey for Thanksgiving; I remember our pumpkin-buying trips in the fall. Think of the things you do every day.

Does your family eat a specific meal together? Is there a regular prayer you say before eating or before going to sleep? These things are tiny, everyday things that added together create our lives. The most amazing thing about God's faithfulness is that it is constant. That may sound redundant, but think about it in regards to your own life. Think of the numerous of small privileges, routines, and traditions that you take for granted. Document and celebrate these things, for they are signs of God's goodness to us.

"There is a time for everything,
and a season for every
activity under heaven."
Ecclesiastes 3:1

Journeying through Special Occasions

Journeying through 6 Special Occasions

For centuries, people have been marking out their journey with special occasions and events. We seem to consider these times - holidays, vacations, etc. - as milestones on our path. This is part of God's ornate design for us as people whom He loves.

He knows the toll a mundane life takes on us. He gave us seasons, and special events to liven things up. In the Scriptures we can easily see how God set up the year to be marked by the festivals and celebrations he established. These festivals were to be repeated year after year in order to remember what God had done for them. They had the Passover in order to remember God's faithfulness in bringing them out of Egypt. I think of special occasions in my own life in the same way; they are a time to remember.

There are some times when you feel the presence of God with you in a unique and poignant way. The day that Laryssa, Audrianna and I got baptized was one of these days - a day of great joy for our entire family.

We have started going to a new church which celebrates believer's baptism and they both wanted to make this statement of their faith. I remembered my own desire and wish that I had been baptized years ago. I prayed, asking the Lord

"The LORD your God is with you, he is mighty to save. He will take great delight in you, he will quiet you with his love, he will rejoice over you with singing." Zephaniah 3:17

When I was a teenager and had made a firm commitment to serving the Lord, my Dad would often ask me if I had ever thought about getting baptized. But I allowed other things to fill my days and before I knew it I was off to college, only attending my home church occasionally. Then as the Lord had planned, I married Bill and became involved in his church which believed in infant baptism. Always in the back of my mind was the wish that I had been baptized when my Dad requested.

Thirty years later my daughters, Laryssa and Audrianna, came to Bill and I with a desire to be baptized.

what I should do and clearly felt called to join them.

What a day of great joy for all us as we walked into the baptismal waters, celebrating all that the Lord had done for each of us and our family. It was a great day for my Dad as well, even though he was not able to join us. He so strongly desired for me to share in the joy of believers making a statement of faith. As the three of us reflect back on this day, we will all remember much more than the date of the event. We will remember the sun shining through rainy skies, the support of our church family and the fact that we have made our public commitment to belong to the Lord.

Laryssa's Baptism

Although it had rained all day, Pastor Jeff told us that he was sure that the weather would clear for the baptism. Sure enough, it sprinkled through the testimonies but when it came time for Laryssa, the first person to walk into the water, the sun broke through. What a blessed experience to be baptized on the same day as my children. I had always put off getting baptized. When Laryssa and Audrianna made the decision to proclaim to the world that Christ is their Savior, it was an honor to do so together as Mother and daughters.

Audrianna's Baptism

Therefore, go and make disciples of all nations, baptizing them in the name of the Father and of the Son and of the Holy Spirit. Matthew 28:19

Certificate of Baptism

Certificate of Baptism

Date: August 3, 2003
Location: Darlington Lake
Darlington, PA
Pastor: Jeff McNicol

One of the special things about the beach is that the combination of sand, sun and water will keep children busy and happy for hours. I've always appreciated the fact that I could sit and relax on the beach while the girls would run back and forth countless of times, each with a new adventure. Their days were full of sand and seashells, little shovels and pails - and smiles. To me, there's nothing more peaceful than sitting on a beach watching the waves roll in, spread over the sand, and flow back out. On a beach vacation, you don't have to hurry to get there before the museum closes, and you don't have to wait in lines. You just prop up your chair, bring a book, and experience peace. We couldn't go to the beach often, and when we did it was a

One tradition in our family was to make the girls' thirteenth birthday a special event. She would get a new dress, and Bill and I would take her out to dinner in Pittsburgh on the night of her birthday. At that time we presented each of them with a purity ring and took the time for them to make a commitment to us and to themselves that they would maintain their purity through the difficult teenage years. It has become a right of passage in our family; it represents growth and maturity - she is no longer a little girl. It represents movement to a new stage in her life and a new stage in her relationship with us. Laryssa's 13th birthday came during the time of our greatest financial struggle. We didn't have the money for this event, but com-

"Then he said to them,
'Come with me by yourselves to a quiet place
and get some rest.'"

Mark 6:31

special treat. Looking back at these pictures, I remember God's faithfulness in providing the means to go. Going to the beach was more than just another vacation; it was a true retreat from everyday life.

mitted to doing it anyway. When I turned 13, my parents gave me a ring; I took that ring and added two small diamonds to it so that it would be unique and special for Laryssa. She seemed appreciative of the fact that I gave her

Peace

I have loved all the days I have ever spent at the beach. The combination of the waves, sun, and sand would keep the girls happy for hours on end and I could dig into a good book. Over and over again, they would fill their pails with water; dig deep in the sand to create sand creations. I am so thankful for all of God's creation, but the ocean is a special refuge for me.

ocean city NJ

beach
fun

SURF & SAND
419

You answer us with *awesome*
deeds of righteousness, O God,
our Savior, the *hope* of all the
ends of the earth and of the
farthest seas. *Psalm 65:5*

the MeRe sense
of living is
JOY
enough!
emily dickinson

JOY

Laryssa's ring

Acts 20:32
Now I commit you to God and to the word of his grace, which can build you up and give you an inheritance among all those who are sanctified.

I Promise

Daddy and I present this ring to you asking you to commit yourself to sexual purity until you get married. This is a big commitment, but one we see as very valuable to every aspect of your life. God will honor your commitment and give you the strength to be able to live it out. We are praying for you every day and for the possible man you may someday marry. We are asking God to keep you both from temptation. We love you very much and are excited to see all that God has planned for you in the future.
Love,
Daddy and Mommy

my ring, and that we continued with this special tradition, regardless of our financial situation. I have always been thankful for her graciousness in accepting a ring that wasn't brand new. She never acted disappointed that only Alycia received a new ring on her birthday. I want this scrapbook page to reflect the importance of this event - it's not just another birthday.

As we look back, God's faithfulness to the girls' through their teenage years is a response to these times of prayer and commitment. This has been an important time in the girls' lives, and I want others to see the motivation behind this occasion.

"For the Lord is good and His love endures forever; His faithfulness continues through all generations."

Psalm 100:5

"I pray that out of His glorious riches He may strengthen you with power through His Spirit in your inner being, so that Christ may dwell in your hearts through faith. And I pray that you, being rooted and established in love, may have power, together with all the saints, to grasp how wide and long and high and deep is the love of Christ, and to know this love that surpasses knowledge - that you may be filled to the measure of all the fullness of God."

Ephesians 3:16-21

Journeying in God's provision

Journeying in God's provision

We tend to think that we have to provide everything for ourselves;
it all comes from us. In reality, the scriptures make it very clear
that the Lord is our provider.

1 Timothy 6:17 commands us to put our hope in the Lord, "who richly provides us with everything for our enjoyment." I think of the Israelites in the desert eating their manna, or Elijah receiving nourishment from the food miraculously brought to him by birds. We spend so much time doubting and worrying. We need to just present God with our needs and trust that He will provide - and He will. On our journey of life, we think we need to plan every detail perfectly. Although we make decisions, God is the one who provides through the twists and turns in the path that we cannot plan for. God provides both the big and small things in life. They are all blessings from Him.

Because of my illness, I often experience a great deal of back pain. I spend a lot of time at the computer, so my chiropractor recommended an ergonomic workstation and chair. I told my husband that I was going to pray about it and God was going to provide a chair for me. Bill told me me a room that had seven or eight chairs, instructing me to choose which one I wanted. I chose a nice one that had the back support I needed, and he told me he wanted to give me the chair for free. I went home, called my husband, and said, "Can you go on your lunch hour and pick up my to just go out and spend the couple hundred dollars. I kept saying, "God's going to provide." When Bill left for work the next morning, he said, "Go and buy a chair today. When I come home, I want to see a chair." I had an appointment at the Small Business Administration that morning, and I asked the man, "You don't happen to have an office chair for sale, do you?" He showed

When Audrianna was a little girl, she had a book entitled A Gift for Grandpa that we enjoyed reading. It told of how through a series of events, God provided exactly what a Grandmother needed.

I learned this lesson when I needed a new office chair for my back. I told Bill that God would provide a new chair for me, but he kept telling me to just go out and buy a new one. When he left for work one morning, he told me to purchase a chair that day. I had an appointment at the Small Business Admin. later that morning and I asked if they happened to have a chair that I could buy. They gave me my pick of several and let me choose a nice one with good back support – at no charge! I called Bill and asked him to please pick up my FREE chair over his lunchtime. It was so much fun to share how God had provided for my needs with the girls as well as to tease Bill.

God always does provide if we allow him to do so!

"God Always Provides"

Gift for GRANDPA

"God Always Provides"

GRANDMA'S TRUST in her heavenly Father never wavers—even when it appears He is providing things she doesn't need, like baby pigs or Smith's Miracle Vitamin Tonic. She knows God will provide a way for her to give Grandpa just the right birthday gift.

YOUNG AND OLD alike will enjoy this story, told through the eyes of Grandpa and Grandma's young grandson.

God provided everything my daughter needed to visit Brazil and more. We had absolutely no way of helping her financially yet she raised all the money that was needed in just a couple of weeks. Every time she had a need arise for this trip, the Lord provided

My Compassion Child

For about a year, I had been praying about whether I should support a Compassion kid. It is something that I've wanted to do. I know that we were going to a Compassion site and I had been praying hard about getting a kid. I found the verse in James in my devotions the night before and I knew that God was calling me to support a kid.

Religion that God our Father accepts as pure and faultless is this: to look after orphans and widows in their distress and to keep oneself from being polluted by the world.
~ James 1:27

We went into a classroom and were told [that] these kids didn't have [sponsors]. I chose this little boy because of his huge, big smile. When I walked [toward] him, he smiled. When I [gave] them my name + address [and] his name, he smiled. I learned that his name is Leonardo de Oliveira. He is 5 years old. I don't know about [his] family situation. He is bright + likes to [play].

Leonardo de Oliveira

I got to paint Leonardo's face. He wanted a heart + a star. The reason his forehead + nose is white is because I gave him a bit of the clown white that was on my face! We wiped it off later!

Alycia chooses Leonardo to sponsor

When she first approached me about applying for this trip, my wish was that I would be able to supply everything she would need to go. Instead the Lord taught our entire family how He provides - all we need to do is His will.

A cheerful look brings joy to the heart.
Proverbs 15:30

This mission trip changed her life, opened her world to the needs of others and brought our daughter home to us a changed 14 year old.

JOY

NAME: ALYCIA
FROM: BRAZIL
TO: PITTSBURGH, PA

CIRCLE OF HUGS

FREE CHAIR that God has provided for me?" It was great fun when the girls came home from school to call them upstairs and say, "Look what God gave me today, out of His Goodness!" So many times, we take the reigns back from

despair. I told her, if God wanted her to go, He would make a way. She applied and was accepted, and then needed to raise about $3,000. I had her put a picture of a thermometer on our refrigerator door, and she sent out a support let-

> "The Lord is gracious and compassionate.
> He provides food for those who fear him;
> He remembers his covenant forever.
> He has shown His people
> the power of His works."
>
> Psalm 111:4-5

God and don't allow him to miraculously provide. Little events and provisions like this exhibit His faithfulness, and by documenting them we encourage our children and grandchildren to trust in His provision.

When my daughter, Alycia, was 13-years-old, she showed me the information for a missions trip to Brazil. We couldn't even afford to buy her envelopes to send out support letters. She was asking if she could go, and I was thinking about the difficult weekend I had just had. I had learned we were in a great deal of debt, and I was at the bottom of

ter. We couldn't even afford to have the letter copied; someone copied it for us as a gift. God not only provided envelopes and stamps; in fact, within three weeks she had the entire amount. God even provided extra for her medical shots and for some clothing she needed for the trip. When others look at pictures of this trip, they need to know the story behind it. I kept thinking how wonderful it would be to just write out a check and send her. However, it was even more wonderful for her to see God's provision first-hand.

Because of all the financial difficulties we have had over the years, we have not been able to save for a college education. During Alycia's senior year of high school, I kept thinking about college coming the next year, and wonder-

"And from your bounty, O God, you provided for the poor."

Psalm 68:10b

ing how we could ever afford to send her. As I worried, I kept asking Bill; he would say, "God's going to provide, Sandy. I don't know how, but God's going to provide."

We always thought she would want to go to a small Christian University, but instead she chose Penn State - the third largest University in the country. She graduated in a high school class of 28 people; sending her off to such a large University was a hard adjustment in my mind. She worked, and paid for what she could. When it came time to send in her acceptance/registration money, I received a check from my brother for $500. He said the stock market had been good to him that year, so he thought he would help out. Between the scholarships Alycia was able to get,

and the low interest loans she gained by going to a State University, God provided remarkably. I got the bill, and when I opened it, I saw a negative number. Now, I'm not the greatest at math so I called Bill to ask him what it meant. When he told me that Penn State owed us money, I was floored. Things kept happening; God kept providing, and we received three checks from Penn State that year. One thing I want to scrapbook about this year is that if we had not allowed her to go where God was calling her, and if she had not been willing to go, God's plan couldn't have been worked out in the same amazing way. God has shown Himself so faithful in providing for my family!

"Remember the wonders He has done..."

Psalm 105:5a

PENN STATE

I will remember the deeds of the Lord; yes I will remember your miracles.
Psalm 77:11

How would we ever be able to pay for college? I wondered this often when Alycia was in her high school years. When I would mention it to Bill, he would always tell me the same thing - "God is going to provide, I don't know how but God's going to provide."

Since Alycia had attended a Christian school throughout her school days, we always assumed that she would attend a Christian College. But after visiting Penn State, one of the largest Universities in the US, she was sure that God was calling her there. After much prayer, the Lord gave us all a peace that that was where she was to go to college.

When the bill came, there was a negative number on the amount due line. I immediately called Bill to ask him what it meant, and he told me that Penn State must owe us money. Because God had called her to a Penn State and she had been a good student, we received more than enough scholarships, grants and loans to pay for her tuition. Throughout her first year, we received 3 refund checks from Penn State. Always will we remember the fact that God provided for her first year at Penn State.

"Remember the former things, those of long ago; I am God, and there is no other; I am God, and there is none like me."

Isaiah 46:9

Journey in God's Grace

Journey in God's Grace

Even as a little girl, I always wanted to be good. I wanted people to like me, and have always been a huge people-pleaser. I have searched for my identity in my number of friends, and how good I was able to be, and others' opinions of me.

But when things didn't go the way I planned, I found out that it is God's goodness, not mine, that gives self-worth. I found grace. God gave me a special friend to show me grace. She didn't care how good my kids were, how I looked, or even if my theology was perfect. She just wanted to be my friend. For the first time, I felt like I could be myself, and she would like me. God's grace is always there - as we travel on our journey. There is so much freedom when you can give up what everyone expects you to do and be what God made you to be. Discover God's grace again today, and revel in it, for it is one of his greatest gifts to us!

I don't need to impress people and I can't do anything to impress you Lord. I just need your grace everyday. This hymn spoke to me through a very broken time in my life when I felt like such a failure at everything I had tried to achieve. Thank you for your wonderful gift of amazing grace.

At a time in my life when I was very broken, I visited my parents' church. I saw an old hymn, one that I remembered singing as a young girl in a country church in rural Pennsylvania. Oh, the words of that song! They were

"The grace of the Lord Jesus be with God's people. Amen."
Revelation 22:21

all about grace - about goodness being all by God's grace. Immediately, I was like a sponge, soaking up the song, deeply drinking it in. I wrote out the song on the back of an offering envelope, word for word, just so I could have it in my hands to remember. Not so I could remember how good I was, how hard I worked, or how many people I pleased. I wanted to remember that only God's grace brings any good to my life. I had to realize that I couldn't make anybody happy, not even myself, but I could accept God's grace. This was a turning point in my spiritual journey. I want everyone to know this is so much more than just a song to me. God used it to show me Himself, and His grace.

In the past few years, Bill and I have been delighting in our ability to fall in love all over again. At one point,

my daughter came to me and said, "this must be what it was like for you and daddy when you were dating." My immediate response was, "No, this is so much better." We had been through horrendous pain and we knew enough about one another to destroy each other. We've seen one another at our very worst. Even after all that, we have had the privi-

"From the fullness of His grace we have all received one blessing after another."
John 1:16

lege of falling in love with each other again. This was only possible through God's faithfulness to us, and our faithfulness to God in sticking it through. We didn't give into the pain, and we worked at it through hard times. The pain wasn't fun, but falling in love with Bill again has been a lot of fun. Ephesians 2:8 states, "For it is by grace you have been saved, through faith — and this not from yourselves, it is the gift of God —." I know it's not the same as salvation, but I always think of Bill when I read that verse, because he is a gift to me from God. God has been so

"...I found the one my heart loves..."
Song of Solomon 3:4

LOVE

Song of Solomon 3:4

I have found

the one my heart loves

Love is patient,
love is kind.
It does not envy,
it does not boast,
it is not proud.
It is not rude,
it is not self-seeking,
it is not easily
angered, it keeps no
record of wrongs.
Love does not delight
in evil but rejoices
with the truth.
It always protects,
always trusts,
always hopes,
always perseveres.
Love never fails

I Corinthians 13:4-8

prayer for our marriage
Jeremiah 32:39
I will give them singleness of heart and action so that they
will always fear me for their own good and the good of their children
after them. 40 I will make an everlasting covenant
with them. I will never stop doing good to them, and I will
inspire them to fear me, so that they will never turn away
from me. 41 I will rejoice in doing them good and will
assuredly plant them in this land.

~Elizabethian Gardens · Roanoke NC · Summer 2002 ~

"His mercy extends to those who fear him,
from generation to generation."

Luke 1:50

faithful to us as a couple, and these pictures of us represent healing and new love given as a gift from our Lord.

God's grace is never-ending, and can lead to many things in our lives. Who knows what door the Lord will be opening in the future? As we travel on our journey, we don't know exactly where it will take us, but we know the faithfulness of our Lord. We know the end of the story; those of us who know Jesus Christ personally, know that in the end we will have ultimate peace and joy in heaven. What a reassuring thought that is! As I look over the events in my life, I see the faithfulness of God traced through it; I am inspired to use scrapbooking as an effective, gratifying, and enjoyable method of communicating this to future generations.

"Love is patient, love is kind.
It does not envy, it does not boast, it is not proud.
It is not rude, it is not self-seeking, it is not easily angered, it keeps no record of wrongs. Love does not delight in evil but rejoices with the truth.
It always protects, always trusts, always hopes, always perseveres.
Love never fails."
1 Corinthians 13: 4-8

HOPE

His mercy extends to those who fear him, from generation to generation. *Luke 1:50*

To those who come after me and want to know what was important to me, I can sum it up in a few words; my God and my family.
I long to greet all of you in heaven so I pray that you will heed to God's calling on your life so we will enjoy eternity together.

He has made everything beautiful in its time. He has also set eternity in the hearts of men; yet they cannot fathom what God has done from beginning to end. Ecclesiastes 3:11

The journey continues...

Scrapbook Design Credit

All scrapbook pages designed in this book used Reminders of Faith™ patterned papers, Chantilly Lace cardstock and vellum, and Ties That Bind™ Fibers unless otherwise noted.

Chapter 1

"Bill's Grandparents" Designed by Corinne French. Font: Gaze Condensed. Ribbon: Offray, Pray Stone: source unknown, Picture box frame: from old file cabinet, Vellum: Paper Gardens.

"Mother's Day Tea" Designed by Beth Beiter. Font: Curlz, Scrap Serif, Gold Oval Frames: source unknown, Teacup: Art Explosion 150,000 Clipart, Buttons: Dress It Up, Ribbon: source unknown, Heart Punch: source unknown.

"My Mom" Designed by Corinne French, Buttons: Dress It Up, Crosses: source unkown.

Chapter 2

"Promise" Designed by Beth Beiter. Font: Papyrus, Beads: source unknown, Heart Punch: Source unknown.

"Lord?" Designed by Chris Pingree. Title: Sizzix, Shadowbox, Dried Flowers: from garden.

"Bill & I" Designed by Chris Pingree, Charms: source unknown.

Chapter 3

"Bill" Designed by Chris Pingree. Font: Brush Script, Tools: source unknown, Buttons: Dress It Up,

"Sandcastles" Designed by Corinne French. Tag by Gina Hurst, Buttons: source unknown.

"My Career" Designed by Marci Whitford. Beads: Bead Treasures, Charms: source unknown.

"Laryssa's Calling" Designed by Beth Beiter Font: Doodle Basic, Scrap Cursive.

Chapter 4

"Alycia" Designed by Beth Beiter, Font: unknown, Heart Glass Shape: Reminders of Faith - Faith Gems, Stones: Dollar Tree.

"Laryssa" Designed by Beth Beiter. Title: QuickCutz, Marissa, Cross: source unknown.

"Audrianna" Designed by Beth Beiter. Font: Scriptina, Heart: source unknown.

"My Dad" Designed by Beth Beiter. Title Sizzix, Shadowbox, Glass Flowers: Reminders of Faith - Faith Gems.

"Always Daddy's Girl" Designed by Chris Pingree, Wire: Artistic Wire, Ribbon: source unknown.

"Special Date" Designed by Beth Beiter. Font: Calligrapher. Ribbon: Offray, Glass Leaves: Dollar Tree enhanced with beads from unknown source.

"Daddy's Girls" Designed by Corinne French. Cardstock Bazzil, Heart: Source unknown.

"Sister's Love" Designed by Marci Whitford. Font: Echelon, Freestyle script, Beads: unkown.

"Love" Designed by Beth Beiter. Title: Quick Cutz, Marissa, Flower Glass Shape: Reminders Of Faith - Faith Gems, Ribbon: source unknown.

Chapter 5

"Sleep" Designed by Marci Whitford. Ribbon: Offray. Font: 2Peas, Ribbons, Mulberry Paper: Lacey Paper Company.

"American Girl" Designed by Marci Whitford. Font: Lucida Handwritting, Buttons: Dress It Up, Girl Punch: MaGill.

"4th of July" Designed by Corinne French, Font: New Times Roman, Bold, Vellum: Strathmore.

"Pumpkins" Designed by Beth Beiter. Font: Doodle Tipsy, Buttons: Dress It Up, Leaves: source unknown,

"Christmas Cookies" Designed by Corinne French. Font Editor Condensed, Navy Cardstock: Paper Garden.

"Christmas 1999" Designed by Beth Beiter. Font: Scrap Cursive. Ribbon: Offray, Buttons: Dress It Up, Deckle Scissors.

Chapter 6

"Baptism" Designed by Corinne French. Cardstock: Bazzil. Font: Californian FB, Vellum: Strathmore.

"Promise" Designed by Marci Whitford. Title: Quick Cutz, Marissa. Font: Scrap Calligraphy, Ribbon: source unknown, Beads: Source Unknown.

"Peace" Designed by Corinne French. Font: Californian FB. Ribbon: Offray.

"Beach" Designed by Corinne French. Font: 2Peas, Vellum: Strathmore.

"Joy" Designed by Corinne French. Font 2Peas, Fallz. Cardstock Bazzil. Tag: Avery.

Chapter 7

"God Always Provides" Designed by Chris Pingre. Cross Charm: source unknown.

"Brazil" Designed by Chris Pingree Title: Paper: source unknown.

"Penn State" Designed by Corinne French, Button: Dress It Up.

Chapter 8

"Grace" Designed by Corinne French. Ribbon: Offray, Journaling: Cordial BLK, Grace Title: New Times Roman, Black Card Stock: Paper Gardens.

"Love" Designed by Marci Whitford. Font: 2Peas, Tom's New Roman, Beads & Charms: source unknown,

"Hope" Designed by Beth Beiter. Font: Celtic Hand, Beads: unknown, Wire: Artistic Wire.

Company Contacts

Ties That Bind
(fiber company)
Gary and Sharon Stone
505-762-0295
www.tiesthatbindfiber.com

Chantilly Lace
(cardstock)
Marc Chabot
866-803-0471
http://www.chantillylacecrafts.com

First Impression Printing
Todd Williams
412-488-3800
Pittsburgh, PA

Reeves Digital Development
(website)
Cindy Reeves
cindy@reevesdigital.com
www.reevesdigital.com

Palermo Imaging
(photography)
Paul Palermo
724-940-0039
www.palermoimaging.com

Hart Photography
Jill Hart Weaver
724-843-1493
New Brighton, PA

www.remindersoffaith.com

"Tell it to your children, and let your children
tell it to their children, and their children
to the next generation."

Joel 1:3

Dear Friends,

"Remember the wonders He has done."
Psalm 105:5

Thank you for traveling through the pages of my spiritual journey. I have enjoyed sharing my scrapbook pages and stories with you. My hope is that you have captured the vision of how you can leave your own stories of God's faithfulness for future generations.

In a recent interview, I was asked if I viewed this book as an evangelistic tool. My answer was a resounding "yes, to this generation and to many generations to come." I can imagine one of my great granddaughters sitting down with my scrapbook only to learn that I had some of the same struggles that she will be going through. She will see that God proved faithful to me, as He will to her. I trust that those to come will see me as a real person not just someone in photos who appears to always be smiling.

As I have studied the scripture, I see God continually calling His people to remember the things He has done:

Trust me when I tell you that in 60 years those that come after you are not going to be concerned with the artistic work you did on your scrapbook pages. However, they will be interested in learning about your life experiences and how God worked in all situations. Now is the time to tell your stories, to leave reminders of your faith for all those who come after you. Please don't wait until you have the perfect workspace or more time, none of us know the number of our days.

I want to hear your stories and see your scrapbook pages. Please share with me at faithinspires@remindersoffaith.com.

Loving my God, my family and my calling,

Sandra L. Joseph

Let me leave you with the verse we started with,

"Set up road signs; put up guideposts. Take note of the highway, the road that you take"
Jeremiah 31:21